MEDITATE THEREIN DAY AND NIGHT

BOOK ONE

I will bless the Lord, who hath given me counsel:
my reins also instruct me in the night seasons.
PSALMS 16:7

J. WESLEY HARVILLE
SHERRIE HOLLIS HARVILLE

PUBLISHED by PARABLES
Earthly Stories with a Heavenly Meaning

Pathways To The Past
Each volume stands alone as an Individual Book
Each volume stands together with others
to enhance the value of your collection

Build your Personal, Pastoral or Church Library
Pathways To The Past contains an ever-expanding list of Christendom's most influencial authors

Augustine of Hippo
Athanasius
E. M. Bounds
John Bunyan
Brother Lawrence
Jessie Penn-Lewis
Bernard of Clairvaux
Andrew Murray
Watchman Nee
Arthur W. Pink
Hannah Whitall Smith
R. A. Torrey
A. W. Tozer
Jean-Pierre de Caussade
Thomas Watson
And many, many more.

Tiitle: Meditate Therein Day And Night
J. Wesley Harville and Sherrie Hollis Harville

ISBN 978-1-945698-00-2
Doctrinal theology
Salvation, Meditation
Meditate Therein Day And Night

MEDITATE THEREIN DAY AND NIGHT

BOOK ONE

I will bless the Lord who hath given me counsel:
my reins also instruct me in the night seasons.
PSALMS 16:7

J. WESLEY HARVILLE
SHERRIE HOLLIS HARVILLE

PUBLISHED by PARABLES
Earthly Stories with a Heavenly Meaning

FOREWORD

Memorize Scripture! The thought still causes a degree of anxiety in me. But this book you hold in your hand helps. The value of God's Word can never be overemphasized, and learning it should never be diminished. Use this book to hide God's book in your heart. Take advantage of the labor of another man who desires to help others labor for the Lord.

In 1979 I met a student at the Missionary Baptist Seminary in Little Rock, Arkansas, who would prove to be a lifelong friend and fellow servant of the Lord Jesus Christ. We shared classes together throughout our seminary days and it did not take long to see that this man was serious about serving the Lord. Wesley Harville was that man. He went on to be a dedicated missionary, loving pastor, and a faithful family man, not necessarily in that order.

Paul Goodwin's Evangelism class caused Wesley to see how memorizing Scripture could help someone hide God's Word in his heart. Wesley and his wife, Sherrie, began to memorize God's Word together. They put together a way to memorize Scripture that worked well for them. Now, Wesley wants to share that system with others.

Today, my friend, Wesley, has experienced the death of his faithful companion, Sherrie. He must suffer from ALS without her by his side, which may be more painful than ALS. Yet, he finds the willpower, determination, and fortitude (known as guts in Arkansas) to do all he can from his wheelchair for the Lord Jesus Christ, whom he deeply loves. This book is a product of that love.

The apostle Paul was arrested and confined, but God used him during that time to write some of the letters in the New Testament. Wesley has now been arrested by ALS and confined to a wheelchair, but God uses him to help others memorize the letters Paul and others wrote in the Bible. It is with great admiration that I recommend to the reader this book that will help you memorize and learn the greatest Book ever written.

Mark T. Thornton
May 25, 2016

APPRECIATION

I do hope and truly pray for you that you feel the importance of the word of God and the urgency of becoming familiar with the book that is called the Holy Bible. I am very thankful for those men and women in my life that encouraged me and taught me in it. I owe so many, a mother who loved the Lord and His word, brothers that are great examples for me of what a Godly man should be and many others who've been examples and teachers. There are two people that I especially want to thank. They are now there with our Lord. One was my instructor in my first year of seminary, Doctor Paul Goodwin taught Bible Analysis and Evangelism. In his Evangelism class we were required to memorize several passages of Scripture every week. Memorization is not one of my strong points. That was very difficult for this (then thirty years) old man. With lots of study I would be ready for that Friday exam. Then at the end of the semester I learned another important lesson, that was that retention is important, too. Thank you Brother Goodwin for sharing your love for this precious Book.

Another person that was a great example and inspiration for me because of her great love of for her Lord and His word is the wonderful and beautiful young lady that chose to share her life with me. I miss her so much. She taught me so much about love. She taught me about loving others and especially about what it is to have a genuine relationship with Jesus Christ. Her love for His word was truly inspiring. She encouraged me to memorize Scripture and she challenged me to join her and we memorized many passages together. She showed me how to use the first letter of each word as an aid to memorizing. What a joy and a privilege it was to worship and grow spiritually with such a sweet, sweet spirited person. No combination of words could ever express how much I miss Sherrie Hollis Harville.

If you say you can't memorize Scripture you are really saying, I am not going to put forth the effort and time that it would take for me to memorize Scripture. You can memorize what you really want to remember. Unless you are suffering from some mental disorder then you can memorize whatever you really want to. You memorized your way to your deer stand, you memorized your way to your favorite shopping center and back home, you memorized the channel numbers of your favorite TV stations and the time & day of your favorite programs, recipes, phone and social security numbers. Your mind is full of what you want to remember. How important is God's word to you? Where is the Bible in the list of your priorities? Thank you Brother Goodwin for really shoving me down the Scripture memory path and thank you Sherrie Harville for making that memory path so much more enjoyable.

This book and the next one in this series contain those verses that Dr. Goodwin required his classes to memorize. These passages are also contained in a booklet that Brother Goodwin wrote, The Memory Path to Blessings. These two volumes follow the same format as others in this series. The pages on the left contain a related quote and the Scripture passage and the page on the right has the acrostic of the Scripture to aid in memorizing the passage..

One more point and then I'll close. (Does that sound like a preacher?) You are now saying, I don't need to memorize Scripture I will always have my Bible right here close and I can pick it up and read it any time I want to. Maybe so, maybe not. I am still a youngster at least I feel like I am and yet this thing called ALS (Lou Gehrig's Disease) will not allow my legs to carry me across the room to pick up my precious Book to read its treasures and if I had my precious Book in front of me my constant companion, ALS, will not let my hands hold it or turn its pages. I am so thankful to those who encouraged me to memorize His word. No my hands don't work anymore and yes I typed this, with my eyes. Today's technology is truly a blessing. I cannot move my arms or legs but I am still me. Please join me in memorizing God's precious word. I would love to have you to join me on the path of memorizing His word. I am adding new passages all the time. It's still not easy for me but it is so worth it. You do not know what is in your future.

"This book of the law shall not depart out of thy mouth; but thou shalt meditate therein day and night, that thou mayest observe to do according to all that is written therein: for then thou shalt make thy way prosperous, and then thou shalt have good success." Joshua 1:8

Also I want to say thank you to the members of Friendship Missionary Baptist Church of Bradford, Arkansas, for their participation in memorizing scripture and encouraging me in the process of developing this course of study.

Love you all, Wesley

Heaven and earth shall pass away: but My words shall not pass away. (Luke 21:33 KJV)

MEDITATE THEREIN DAY AND NIGHT

Verses from Dr. Paul Goodwin's

THE MEMORY PATH TO BLESSINGS

Part 1

This book of the law shall not depart out of thy mouth;
but thou shalt meditate therein day and night,
that thou mayest observe to do according to all that is written therein:
for then thou shalt make thy way prosperous,
and then thou shalt have good success.
Joshua 1:8 (KJV)

Isn't it amazing that no matter what you do you can't get that silly song out of your head? You try everything that you can think of to move on to something else but that song is still there. Try another song for a while, reading something, poetry, or anything but before you know it you are humming that same ole song again.

Wouldn't it be great if God's Word would stick like that music did? Wouldn't it be great if those great passages of Scripture were going over and over in your head like that silly song?

You probably worked to memorize the words of that silly song or you heard that tune over and over again before it became lodged forever in your mind. Well that same principle will work for Scripture as well. You can memorize God's Word if you really want to. You have already memorized many addresses, phone numbers, names, formulas, recipes, and probably some Scripture. You can memorize if you really want to.

As Dr. Paul Goodwin said,

"People usually remember what they are interested in. A lack of interest usually equals bad memory work. Much depends on one's attitude. The more interest there is the more power there is to memorize.

Memorizing Scripture is a good work, and you can count on God to help you. "I can do all things through Christ which strengtheneth me" (Philippians 4:13).

Let us begin with confidence this exciting adventure in the Word of God."[1]

[1] Goodwin, Paul, The Memory Path to Blessings, 1980 p14 Publisher unknown

WHY MEMORIZE GOD'S WORD?

Because we are commanded to

It is not just a good idea to study and memorize God's Word, we are commanded to do so. In more than one instance God commands us to get His word in our heads and hearts (Deuteronomy 6:6-9; 11:18-21; Joshua 1:7-8; Psalm 37:28-31; 119:9-11).

6 And these words, which I command thee this day, shall be in thine heart: 7 And thou shalt teach them diligently unto thy children, and shalt talk of them when thou sittest in thine house, and when thou walkest by the way, and when thou liest down, and when thou risest up. 8 And thou shalt bind them for a sign upon thine hand, and they shall be as frontlets between thine eyes. 9 And thou shalt write them upon the posts of thy house, and on thy gates. (Deuteronomy 6:6-9 KJV)

God's Word in your heart will protect you from sin and folly

We need the Word of God in our minds to assist us when facing temptation. God's Word teaches us how to resist sin and foolishness, why we should do so, and what will happen if we don't. It teaches us how to do what God commands us to do.

Jesus used Scripture to defeat Satan (Matthew 4:1-11). David says that God's Word in your heart will keep your feet from slipping (Psalm 37:28-31). The Psalmist says in Psalm 119:9-11 that knowing God's Word is the key to purity. And Paul says that Scripture is a sword to use against the wiles of the devil (Ephesians 6:13-18).

How can God's Holy Spirit protect us if we do not have His Word in our minds? We must study it, memorize it, and meditate on it!

God's Word in your heart will cleanse you from sin and folly

Whatever you put into your mind will determine what you think about and what you think about will determine what you do - whether for good or bad (Deuteronomy 30:14: Proverbs 15:14). Meditation on the Scriptures cleanses and transforms the mind (Romans 12:1-2) and heart (Proverbs 4:23). God's Word will help erase the bad programming in your head. It cleans out garbage and filth and makes room for the beautiful, the character of Christ. Memorizing

God's Word will cleanse your heart and will make a great impact on your life. Therefore, meditate on it day and night. These are great reasons to memorize Scripture.

To put it in modern technical terms, it is sad today that many Christian's hard drives are filled with useless data. We need to start downloading Scripture now. Then the Holy Spirit will have data to access in our time of need.

God's Word in your heart will help us find the answer to life's questions

"The Bible is Heaven's Answer Book to earth's questions. One verse of Scripture memorized and meditated upon often provides answers to many perplexing questions. " [2]

God's Word in your heart will increase your love for its Author

"The more we love the Word the more we love its Author." [3]

[2] Goodwin, Paul, The Memory Path to Blessings, 1980 p7, Publisher unknown.

[3] Ibid, p6.

HOW TO MEMORIZE GOD'S WORD

You must get started

Most of us are very busy and we will find it hard to get a-round-to-it. That first step is always the hardest. If you want to run, you have to get up off the couch, and start to run. Even if you only run a short distance you have to start. The same applies to memorizing God's Word. You have to set aside time. You must plan and organize a schedule. You have to choose a passage and then memorize it.

If you desire to learn more than a few verses, then your memorization work must be a priority in your life. You may have to set some other things aside to make the time. Memorizing scripture should become a part of your everyday life. It must become extremely important to you. Remember that this will lead to a deeper relationship with Christ that should make it immensely important.

You must learn the verses with 100% accuracy

Make it your goal to learn the verses that you learn flawlessly, strive for 100% accuracy. Take as much time as is necessary for you to get the passages right. Quality is more desirable than quantity.

You must review (use what you have learned)

If you hope to make the memorizing of scripture a long-term, continuing part of your life, you will find that review will take more time than the learning of new verses. This thought can be disturbing if you are the kind of person who likes to keep things moving forward. You may want to memorize new verses each day and review gets in the way. Such an attitude is not wise. The result is a large quantity of scripture that is so poorly learned that after a few weeks, it cannot be recalled with any reliability.

Review is an important part of a successful scripture memory program.

Each set of verses you learn must be completely mastered before you go on to the next.

Review your verses at least once each day for at least two months. It is best if you can review them several times a day. Don't think that rehearsing them two or three times a day for two months is too much. It is not. In fact, much practice is essential if you are going to be successful in the long run. You may be able to memorize a passage quickly, but it will not become a part of your permanent memory until it has been reviewed over and over many times. A passage of scripture will not be successfully memorized until you have reviewed it at least 100 times.

Each week you will add a few verses to what you know. Each week you have to spend time learning your new material and reviewing what you have recently learned.

TIPS FOR MEMORIZING GOD'S WORD

(How to use this book)

There are many ways to memorize. You may want to start a notebook with the verses that you are memorizing printed in it. Writing the verses is a great way to memorize them. Or you may want to print them on index cards and carry them with you reviewing them as you have opportunity. However you decide to memorize the verses that you select it is important to recite them out loud as much as you can. That helps you to get the passage into your mind and helps you to check yourself to see if you are getting the passage right.

A great way to memorize is to read the passage over several times then looking only at the first letters of each word try to say the passage. In this book you will find a number of passages that are printed out with the facing pages containing the first letter of each word.

Read the verse several times, at least six or eight times. Then turn the page over and looking at the acrostic (the letters) on the next page. Recite the verse until it becomes so familiar that you only need to look at the reference and you can correctly quote the passage.

Once that you have learned this passage it is important to review it over and over to make it permanent in your mind. You may feel like you are over learning the passage but you will find that later on the passage will be easier to recall. Even then it cannot be stressed too much that review is necessary. Go back to it over and over for many months, in fact you should never stop reviewing it. As time goes on you will not have to review it as often. At some later time if you have any problem reciting the passage then retrieve this book and reestablish it in your mind.

REVIEW. REVIEW. REVIEW

Always:

1. Say the scripture reference then
2. quote the verse then
3. say the scripture reference again.

(Address . . . Verse . . . Address)

This will help you to link the passage with the reference.

To obey God's Word is far more important than to memorize it. Do not look down on others because you know large quantities of Scripture. The person that has not memorized any Scripture but obeys God is much better off than the one who has memorized great portions, but has experienced no life changes.

Now may be a good time to say that you do not need to memorize scripture to be a Christian. You need a personal relationship with the person of Jesus Christ. You do not have to memorize scripture to be a godly person. So, if you choose not to memorize Scripture, that does not make you a better or worse Christian than someone who does. On the other hand, because of its power you do need an understanding of God's Word. You owe it to yourself to learn as much of His Word as you can.

Your godliness is your own responsibility!

3 According as His divine power hath given unto us all things that pertain unto life and godliness, through the knowledge of Him that hath called us to glory and virtue: 4 Whereby are given unto us exceeding great and precious promises: that by these ye might be partakers of the divine nature, having escaped the corruption that is in the world through lust. 5 And beside this, giving all diligence, add to your faith virtue; and to virtue knowledge; 6 And to knowledge temperance; and to temperance patience; and to patience godliness; 7 And to godliness brotherly kindness; and to brotherly kindness charity. 8 For if these things be in you, and abound, they make you that ye shall neither be barren nor unfruitful in the knowledge of our Lord Jesus Christ. 9 But he that lacketh these things is blind, and cannot see afar off, and hath forgotten that he was purged from his old sins. 10 Wherefore the rather, brethren, give diligence to make your calling and election sure: for if ye do these things, ye shall never fall: 11 For so an entrance shall be ministered unto you abundantly into the everlasting kingdom of our Lord and Saviour Jesus Christ.

(II Peter 1:3-11 KJV)

LESSON 1

Life is short, uncertain and death is sure.
Job 14:1, 2

Benjamin Franklin
1706 - 1790
The body of Benjamin Franklin, Printer, lies here, food for worms; but the work shall not be lost, for it will appear once more in a new and more elegant edition, revised and corrected by the Author.

Job 14:1, 2

1 ***Man that is born of a woman is of few days, and full or Trouble.***
2 ***He cometh forth like a flower, and is cut down: he fleeth also as a shadow, and continueth not.***

Read it, read it, read it and read it again.

Hint: Always say the address before and after saying the passage. The passage address is where the passage is found in the Bible, (the Scripture reference). In this case it's Job 14:1 & 2.

Job 14:1, 2

1 ***M T I B O A W I O F***
D, A F O T.
2 ***H C F L A F, A I C D:***
H F A A A S, A C N.

Say the passage until you can quote it without looking at this aid.

Life is short, uncertain and death is sure.
Proverbs 27:1

Steve Jobs
1955 – 2011

"If you live each day as it was your last, someday you'll most certainly be right"

Proverbs 27:1

1 Boast not thyself of tomorrow; for thou knowest not what a day may bring forth.

Read this passage until you feel you are familiar with it.

Proverbs 27:1

1 B N T O T; F T K N W A D M B F.

Say the passage until you can quote it from only the address.

Life is short, uncertain and death is sure.

James 4:13, 14

Ernest Hemingway

1899 – 1961

"Madame, all stories, if continued far enough, end in death, and he is no true-story teller who would keep that from you."

James 4:13, 14

13 Goto now, ye that say.
To day or to morrow we will go into such a city, and continue there a year, and buy and sell, and get gain:
14 Whereas ye know not what shall be on the morrow. For what is your life? It is even a vapour, that appeareth for a little time, and then vanisheth away.

Read these verses several times before moving to the memory aid on the next page.

Life is short, uncertain and death is sure
James 4:13, 14

James 4:13, 14

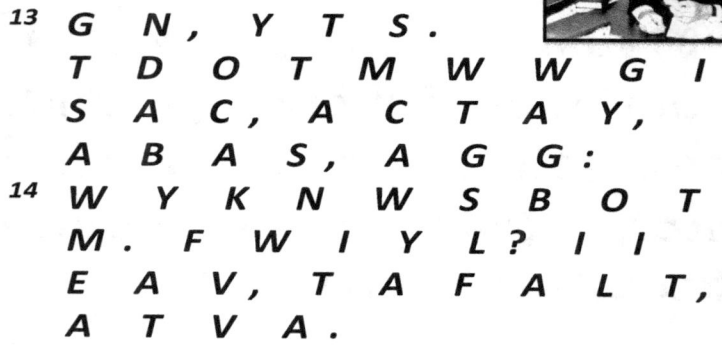

13 G N, Y T S.
T D O T M W W G I
S A C, A C T A Y,
A B A S, A G G:
14 W Y K N W S B O T
M. F W I Y L? I I
E A V, T A F A L T,
A T V A.

Say the passage until you can quote it from only the address..

Life is short, uncertain and death is sure
Hebrews 9:27

They, then, who are destined to die, need not be careful to inquire what death they are to die, but into what place death will usher them.

Augustine
354 - 430 AD

Hebrews 9:27

27 *And as it is appointed unto men once to die, but after this the judgment:*

Life is short, uncertain and death is sure Life is short, uncertain and death is sure

Hebrews 9:27

27 ***A A I I A U M O T D, B A T T J:***

Review . . . Review . . . Review ! ! !

LESSON 2

God is holy.
Psalm 99:9

God cannot change for the better, for He is already perfect; and being perfect, He cannot change for the worse.

Arthur W. Pink
1886 - 1952

Psalm 99:9

9 ***Exalt the Lord our God, and worship at His holy hill; for the Lord our God Is holy.***

Preview Psalm 99:9 here.

Psalm 99:9

9 *E T L O G, A*
W A H H H; F
T L O G I H.

Download Psalm 99:9 to your memory bank here.

God is holy.
Psalm 145:17

Arthur W. Pink
1886 - 1952
The Attributes of God

"Power is God's hand or arm, omniscience His eye, mercy His bowels, eternity His duration, but holiness is His beauty" (S. Charnock). It is this, supremely, which renders Him lovely to those who are delivered from sin's dominion."

Psalm 145:17

17 ***The LORD is righteous in all His ways, and holy in all His works.***

Psalm 145:17

17 ***T L I R I A H W,***
A H I A H W.

. . . a workman that needeth not to be ashamed.

Life is short, uncertain and death is sure
Isaiah 57:15

Arthur W. Pink
1886 – 1952

To the one who delights in the sovereignty of God the clouds not only have a 'silver lining' but they are silvern all through, the darkness only serving to offset the light!

Isaiah 57:15

15 For thus saith the high and lofty One that inhabiteth eternity, whose name is Holy; I dwell in the high and holy place, with him also that is of a contrite and humble spirit, to revive the spirit of the humble, and to revive the heart of the contrite ones.

Read it, read it, read it and read it again.

Isaiah 57:15

15 *F T S T H A L O T*
I E, W N I H; I D
I T H A H P, W H
A T I O A C A H S,
T R T S O T H, A
T R T H O T C O.

Say it, say it, say it again and quote it.

God is holy.
Habakkuk 1:13

Arthur W. Pink
1886 – 1952

Divine sovereignty is not the sovereignty of a tyrannical Despot, but the exercised pleasure of One who is infinitely wise and good! Because God is infinitely wise He cannot err, and because He is infinitely righteous He will not do wrong.

Habakkuk 1:13

13 ***Thou art of purer eyes than to behold evil, and canst not look on iniquity...***

Habakkuk 1:13

13 *T A O P E T T B E, A C N L O I ...*

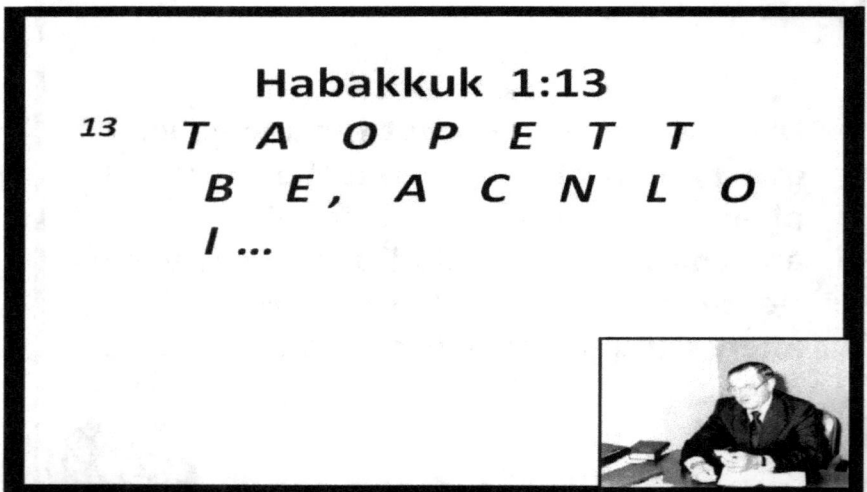

There is no better use of time than reading God's word

LESSON 3

Man was made in the image of God, but through transgression fell.
Genesis 1:27

What can be more foolish than to think that all this rare fabric of heaven and earth could come by chance, when all the skill of art is not able to make an oyster!

Jeremy Taylor
1613 - 1667

Genesis 1:27

27 *So God created man in His own image, in the image of God created He him; male and female created He them.*

God created you with intellect so you can read His word.

Genesis 1:27

27 S G C M I H O I, I T I O G C H H; M A F C H T.

God created you with a mind to experience His word.

Man was made in the image of God, but through transgression fell.
Genesis 1:31

J. I. Packer

The unceasing activity of the Creator, whereby in overflowing bounty and goodwill, He upholds His creatures in ordered existence, guides and governs all events, circumstances, and free acts of angels and men, and directs everything to its appointed goal, for His own glory.

Genesis 1:31

31 ***And God saw every thing that He had made, and, behold, it was very good. And the evening and the morning were the sixth day.***

If you can read and don't what advantage have you on the unlearned?

Genesis 1:31

31 ***A G S E T T H H M, A, B, I W V G. A T E A T M W T S D.***

Fill your mind with the "mind of Christ."

Man was made in the image of God, but through transgression fell.
Romans 5:12

Charles Hodge
1797 – 1878

Original sin is the only rational solution of the undeniable fact of the deep, universal and early manifested sinfulness of men in all ages, of every class, and in every part of the world.

Romans 5:12

12 *Wherefore, as by one man sin entered into the world, and death by sin; and so death passed upon all men, for that all have sinned:*

If Satan can't make bad he'll make you busy.
Make time to read God's word.

Romans 5:12

12 ***W, A B O M S E***
I T W, A D B S;
A S D P U A M,
F T A H S:

Your mind is agift from God and it is a terrible thing to waste.

Man was made in the image of God, but through transgression fell.
Romans 5:19

Martin Luther
1483 - 1546

Original sin is in us, like the beard. We are shaved today and look clean, and have a smooth chin; tomorrow our beard has grown again, nor does it cease growing while we remain on earth. In like manner original sin cannot be extirpated from us; it springs up in us as long as we live. Nevertheless we are bound to resist it to our utmost strength, and to cut it down unceasingly.

Read . . . Read . . . Read

Romans 5:19

19 *For as by one man's disobedience many were made sinners, so by the obedience of one shall many be made righteous.*

Read . . . Read . . . Read

Romans 5:19

19 ***F A B O M D***
M W M S, S B
T O O O S M
B M R.

Review . . . Review. . . Review

LESSON 4

All persons are sinners.

Psalm 14:2, 3

Augustine

354 - 430 AD

I inquired what iniquity was, and found it to be no substance, but the perversion of the will, turned aside from Thee, O God, the Supreme, towards these lower

Psalm 14:2, 3

2 The Lord looked down from heaven upon the children of men, to see if there were any that did understand, and seek God. 3 They are all gone aside, they are all together become filthy: there is none that doeth good, no, not one.

Read this passage until you feel you are familiar with it.

Psalm 14:2, 3

2 *T L L D F H U T C*
O M, T S I T W A T
D U, A S G.
3 *T A A G A, T A A T*
B F: T I N T D G,
N, N O.

Say the passage until you can quote it without looking at this aid.

All persons are sinners.
Ecclesiastes 7:20

Author unknown

Temptation usually comes in through a door that has deliberately been left open.

Ecclesiastes 7:20

20 *For there is not a just man upon earth, that doeth good, and sinneth not.*

Read these verses several times
before moving to the memory aid on the next page.

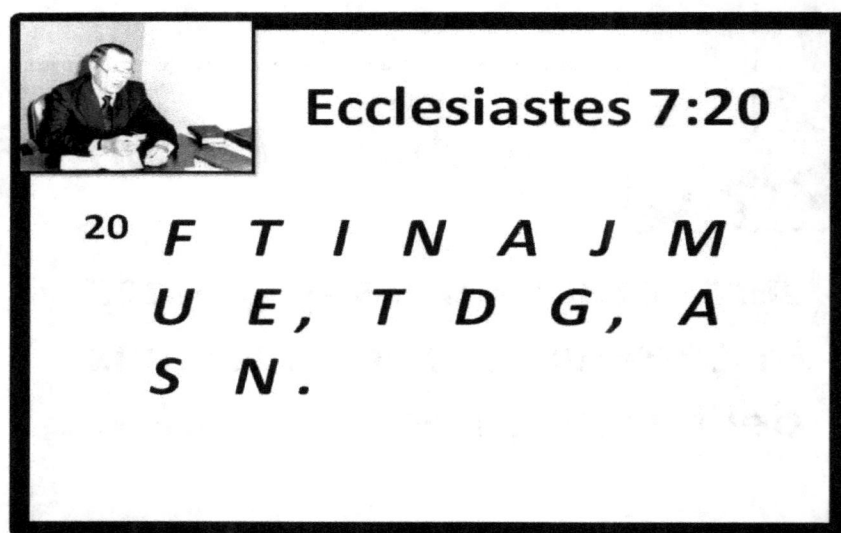

Ecclesiastes 7:20

20 ***F T I N A J M U E, T D G, A S N.***

Say the passage until you can quote
it from only the address.

All persons are sinners.
Romans 3:10-12

C. S. Lewis

1898 – 1963

All men alike stand condemned, not by alien codes of ethics, but by their own, and all men therefore are conscious of guilt.

Romans 3:10-12

10 As it is written. There is none right-
eous, no, not one: 11 There is none that
understandeth, there is none that seek-
eth after God. 12 They are all gone out
of the way, they are together become
unprofitable: there is none that doeth
good, no, not one.

Address-verse-address . . . Address-verse-address . . .

Romans 3:10-12

10 *A I I W. T I N R,*
N, N O:
11 *T I N T U, T I N T*
S A G.
12 *T A A G O O T W,*
T A T B U: T I N
T D G, N, N O.

Address-verse-address . . . Address-verse-address . . .
Address-verse-address . . .

All persons are sinners.
Romans 3:23

C. S. Lewis

1898 - 1963

We have a strange illusion that mere time cancels sin. But mere time does nothing either to the fact or to the guilt of a sin.

Romans 3:23

23 For all have sinned, and come short of the glory of God;

Preview Romans 3:23 here.

Review . . . Review . . . Review ! ! !

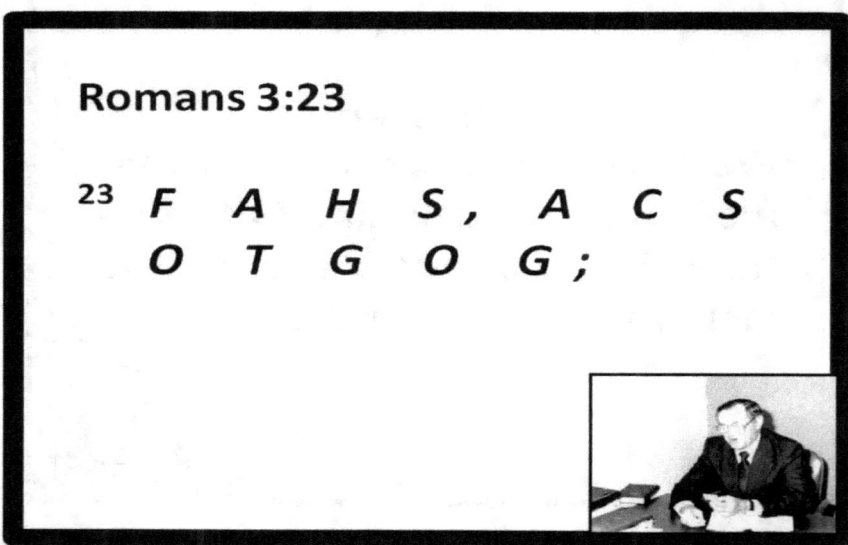

Romans 3:23

23 ***F A H S , A C S O T G O G ;***

Download Romans 3:23 to your memory here.

LESSON 5

The consequences of sin are serious.

Luke 16:24

Charles H. Spurgeon

1834 - 1892

As the salt flavors every drop in the Atlantic, so does sin affect every atom of our nature. It is so sadly there, so abundantly there, that if you cannot detect it, you are deceived.

Luke 16:24

24 ***And he cried and said. Father Abraham, have mercy on me, and send Lazarus, that he may dip the tip of his finger in water, and cool my tongue; for I am tormented in this flame.***

Study to shew thyself approved unto God . . .

Luke 16:24

24 ***A H C A S. F A, H***
M O M, A S L, T H
M D T T O H F I
W, A C M T; F I A
T I T F.

. . . a workman that needeth not to be ashamed.

The consequences of sin are serious.
Romans 6:23

Alexander MacLaren
1826 – 1910

Embrace in one act the two truths– thine own sin, and God's infinite mercy in Jesus Christ.

Romans 6:23

23 ***For the wages of sin is death; but the gift of God is eternal life through Jesus Christ our Lord.***

Romans 6:23

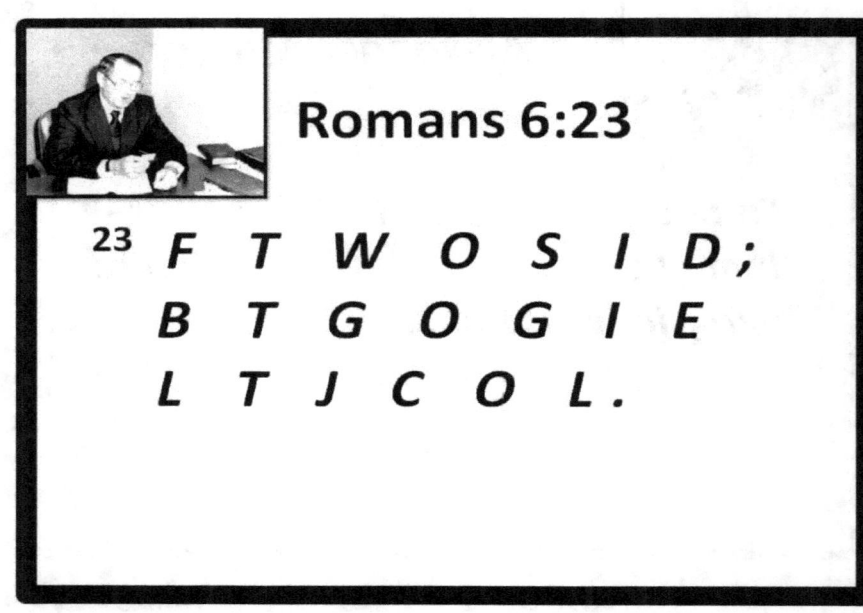

23 ***F T W O S I D;***
B T G O G I E
L T J C O L.

Say it, say it, say it again and quote it.

The consequences of sin are serious.
Galatians 6:7

John Bunyan
1628 - 1688
Source: A Puritan Golden Treasury

Sin is the dare of God's justice, the rape of His mercy, the jeer of His patience, the slight of His power, and the contempt of His love.

Galatians 6:7

7 ***Be not deceived; God is not mocked: for whatsoever a man soweth, that shall he also reap.***

There is no better use of time than reading God's word.

Galatians 6:7

7 B N D; G I N M: F W A M S, T S H A R.

There is nothing better to fill your mind with than God's word.

The consequences of sin are serious.
Revelation 21:8

Billy Sunday
1862 – 1935

Hell is the highest reward that the devil can offer you for being a servant of his.

Revelation 21:8
[8] ***But the fearful, and unbelieving, and the abominable, and murderers, and whoremongers, and sorcerers, and idolaters, and all liars, shall have their part in the lake which burneth with fire and brimstone: which is the second death.***

God created you with intellect so you can read His word.

Review . . . Review . . . Review ! ! !

Revelation 21:8

8 *B T F, A U, A T A, A M, A W, A S, A I, A A L, S H T P I T L W B W F A B: W I T S D.*

There is nothing better to fill your mind with than God's word.

LESSON 6

Even though we are sinners God loves us.
John 3:16

C. S. Lewis
1898 - 1963
The great thing to remember is that though our feelings come and go God's love for us does not.

John 3:16
16 ***For God so loved the world, that He gave His only begotten Son, that whosoever belleveth in Him should not perish, but have everlasting life.***

If you can read and don't what advantage have you on the unlearned?

John 3:16

16 ***F G S L T W, T H***
G H O B S, T W
B I H S N P, B H
E L.

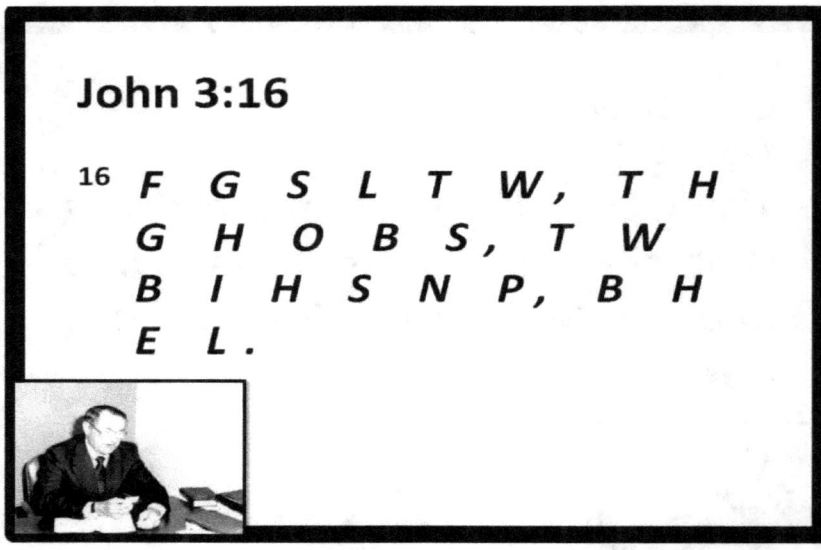

God created you with a mind to remember His word.

Even though we are sinners God loves us.
Romans 5:8

Augustine
354 -430 AD

God loves each of us as if there were only one of us.

Romans 5:8

8 ***But God commendeth His love toward us, in that, while we were yet sinners, Christ died for us.***

If Satan can't make bad he'll make you busy.
Make time to read God's word.

Romans 5:8

8 ***B G C H L T U, I T, W W W Y S, C D F U.***

Fill your mind with the "mind of Christ."

Even though we are sinners God loves us.
I John 4:10

Unknown Author

Whom should we love, if not Him who loved us, and gave Himself for us?

I John 4:10

10 ***Herein is love, not that we loved God, but that He loved us, and sent His Son to be the propitiation for our sins.***

Read . . . Read . . . Read

I John 4:10

10 *H I L, N T W L G, B T H L U, A S H S T B T P F O S.*

Your mind is a gift from God and it is a terrible thing to waste.

Even though e are sinners God loves us.
John 4:19

C. S. Lewis
1898 - 1963

He loved us not because we are lovable, but because He is love.

John 4:19

19 ***We love Him, because He first loved us.***

Read this passage until you feel you are familiar with it.

Review . . . Review . . . Review ! ! !

John 4:19

19 *W L H, B H*
F L U.

Say the passage until you can quote it without looking at this aid.

LESSON 7

Christ is God and He came into the world to save sinners.

John 1:1-3

J. Sidlow Baxter

1903 - 1999

Fundamentally, our Lord's message was Himself. He did not come merely to preach a Gospel; He Himself is that Gospel. He did not come merely to give bread; He said, "I am the bread." He did not come merely to shed light; He said, "I am the light." He did not come merely to show the door; He said, "I am the door." He did not come merely to name a shepherd; He said, "I am the shepherd." He did not come merely to point the way; He said, "I am the way, the truth, and the life."

John 1:1-3

1 In the beginning was the Word, and the Word was with God, and the Word was God. 2 The same was in the beginning with God. 3 All things were made by Him; and without Him was not any thing made that was made.

Read these verses several times before moving to the memory aid on the next page.

John 1:1-3

1 *I T B W T W, A T*
W W W G, A T W
W G.
2 *T S W I T B W G.*
3 *A T W M B H; A*
W H W N A T M
T W M.

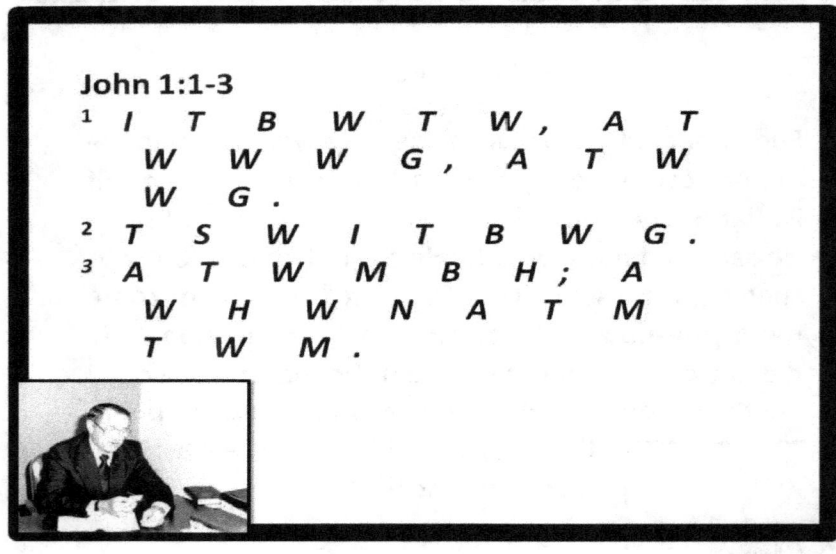

Say the passage until you can quote it from only the address.

Christ is God and He came into the world to save sinners.
John 1:14

Unknown Author

Buddha never claimed to be God. Moses never claimed to be Jehovah. Mohammed never claimed to be Allah. Yet Jesus Christ claimed to be the true and living God. Buddha simply said, "I am a teacher in search of the truth." Jesus said, "I am the Truth." Confucius said, "I never claimed to be holy." Jesus said, "Who convicts Me of sin?" Mohammed said, "Unless God throws His cloak of mercy over me, I have no hope." Jesus said, "Unless you believe in Me, you will die in your sins."

John 1:14

14 And the Word was made flesh, and dwelt among us, (and we beheld His glory, the glory as of the only begotten of the Father,) full of grace and truth.

Address-verse-address . . . Address-verse-address . . .
Address-verse-address . . .

John 1:14

14 **A T W W M F,**
A D A U, (A W
B H G, T G A
O T O B O T
F,) F O G A T.

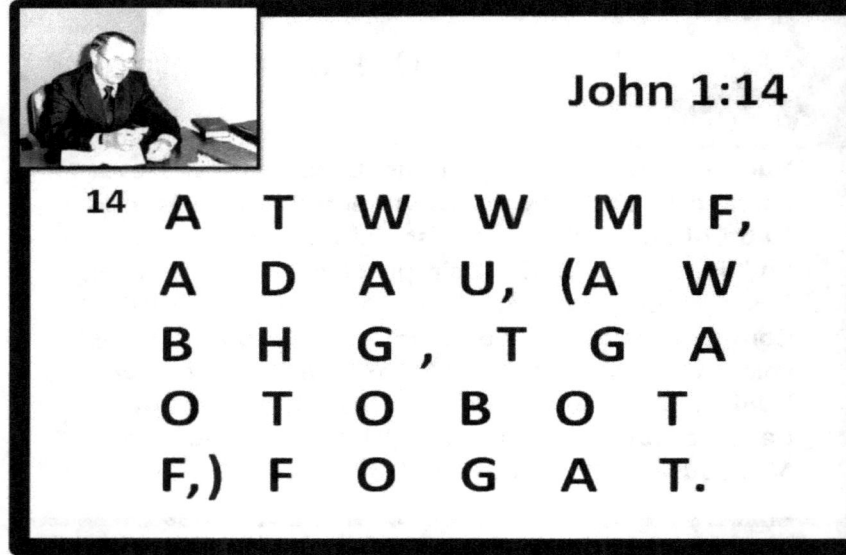

Address-verse-address . . . Address-verse-address . . .
Address-verse-address . . .

Christ is God and He came into the world to save sinners.
Luke 19:10

Augustine

354 - 430 AD

I have read in Plato and Cicero sayings that are very wise and very beautiful; but I never read in either of them: "Come unto Me all ye that labour and are heavy laden."

Luke 19:10

10 ***For the Son of Man is come to seek and to save that which was lost.***

Preview Luke 19:10 here.

Luke 19:10

10 *F T S O M I*
C T S A T S
T W W L.

Download Luke 19:10 to your memory here.

Christ is God and He came into the world to save sinners.
I Timothy 1:15

Albert Einstein

1879 - 1955

As a child I received instruction both in the Bible and in the Talmud. I am a Jew, but I am enthralled by the luminous figure of the Nazarene....No one can read the Gospels without feeling the actual presence of Jesus. His personality pulsates in every word. No myth is filled with such life.

I Timothy 1:15

15 ***This is a faithful saying, and worthy of all acceptation, that Christ Jesus came into the world to save sinners; of whom I am chief.***

Review . . . Review . . . Review ! ! !

I Timothy 1:15

15 *T I A F S, A W*
O A A, T C J
C I T W T S S;
O W I A C.

. . a workman that needeth not to be ashamed.

LESSON 8

Christ is not a sinner.

Matthew 1:18

Sholem Asch

1880 - 1957

Jesus Christ is to me the outstanding personality of all time, all history, both as Son of God and as Son of Man. Everything He ever said or did has value for us today and that is something you can say of no other man, dead or alive. There is no easy middle ground to stroll upon. You either accept Jesus or reject Him.

Matthew 1:18

18 Now the birth of Jesus Christ was on this wise: When as His mother Mary was espoused to Joseph, before they came together, she was found with Child of the Holy Ghost.

Read it, read it, read it and read it again.

Matthew 1:18

18 N T B O J C W
O T W: W A H M
M W E T J, B T C
T, S W F W C O T
H G.

Say it, say it, say it again and quote it.

Christ is not a sinner.
Matthew 27:19

Adrian Rogers
1931-2005

He took upon humanity, He is now a man. He is God of very God. He is the resurrected Christ with humanity that is ever His. He will be and is forever like me and when I see Him I will be forever like Him.

Matthew 27:19

19 When he was set down on the judgment seat, his wife sent unto him, saying, Have thou nothing to do with that just Man: for I have suffered many things this day in a dream because of Him.

There is no better use of time than reading God's word.

Matthew 27:19

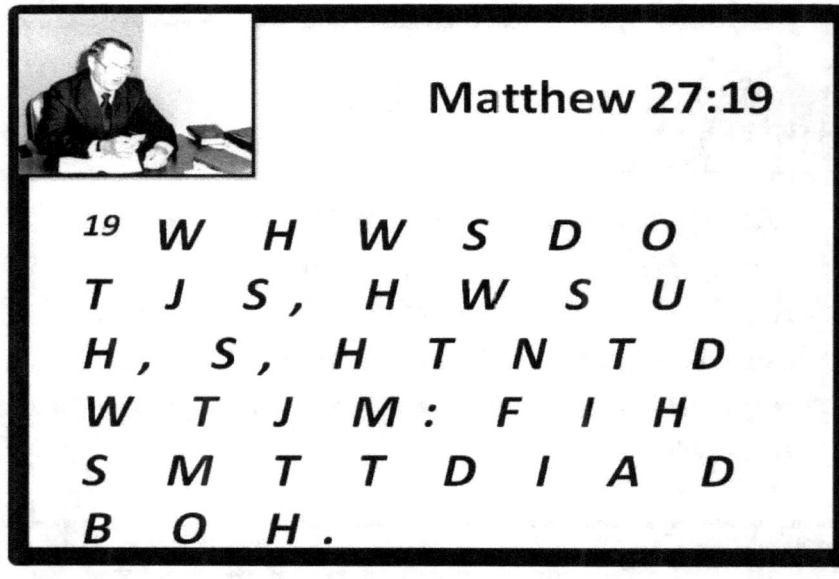

19 W H W S D O
T J S, H W S U
H, S, H T N T D
W T J M: F I H
S M T T D I A D
B O H.

There is nothing better to fill your mind with than God's word.

Christ is not a sinner.
Luke 23:14

Fyodor Dostoyevsky
1821 – 1881

Even those who have renounced Christianity and attack it, in their inmost being still follow the Christian ideal, for hitherto neither their subtlety nor the ardour of their hearts has been able to create a higher ideal of man and of virtue than the ideal given by Christ of old.

Luke 23:14

14 ***I... have found no fault in this Man...***

God created you with intellect so you can read His word.

Luke 23:14

14 *I . . . H F N F*
I T M . . .

There is nothing better to fill your mind with than God's word.

Christ is not a sinner.
Matthew 27:4

Henry Allen Ironside
1876 - 1951

When the Lord Jesus Christ became my surety ... He went to Calvary's cross, and all my guilt was charged against Him. He settled for everything, and then He cried, 'It is finished.' And on the basis of that finished work, God can freely forgive, and justify completely, every poor sinner who trusts in the Lord Jesus Christ.

Matthew 27:4

4 ***Saying, I have sinned In that I have betrayed the innocent blood. And they said, What is that to us? see thou to that.***

If you can read and don't what advantage have you on the unlearned?

Matthew 27:4

4 ***S, I H S I T I***
H B T I B. A T
S, W I T T U?
S T T T.

God created you with a mind to remember His word.

Christ is not a sinner.
Luke 23:41

John R. Rice
1895 - 1980

When you get saved, you get saved not because you deserve it, but because you simply let God save you and because you confess your own poor sinful state and your inability to save yourself.

Luke 23:41

41 ***And we indeed justly; for we receive the due reward of our deeds: but this Man hath done nothing amiss.***

If Satan can't make bad he'll make you busy.
Make time to read God's word.

Review . . . Review . . . Review ! ! !

Luke 23:41

41 *A W I J; F W*
R T D R O O
D: B T M H D
N A.

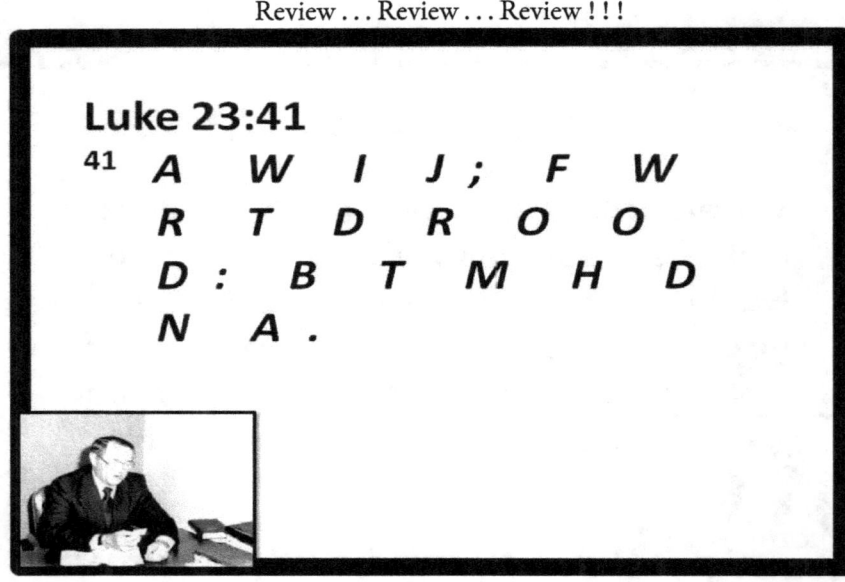

Fill your mind with the "mind of Christ."

LESSON 9

Christ is not a sinner.
John 8:46

Augustine

354 - 430 AD

Where I found truth, there found I my God, Who is the truth itself.

John 8:46

46 ***Which of you convinceth Me of sin? And if I say the truth, why do ye not believe Me?***

Read . . . Read . . . Read

John 8: 46

46 ***W O Y C M***
O S? A I I S
T T, W D Y
N B M?

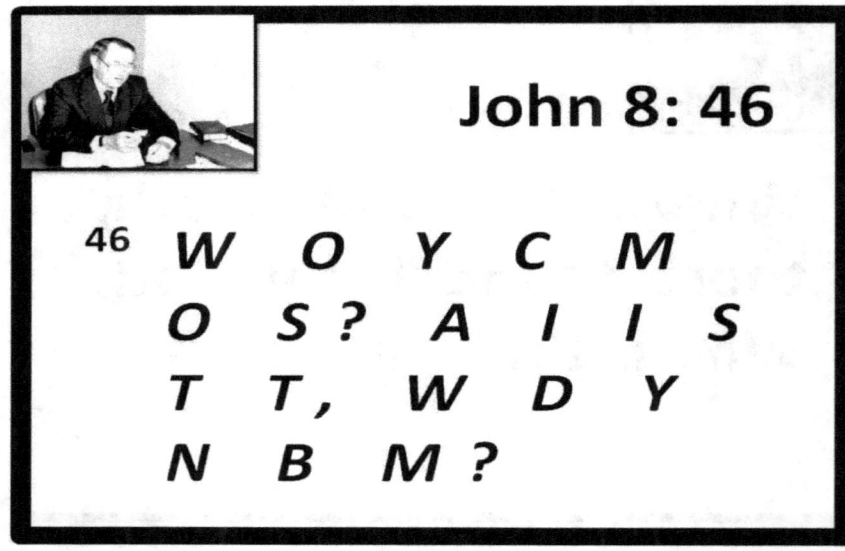

Your mind is a gift from God and it is a terrible thing to waste.

Christ is not a sinner.
Hebrews 4:15

Unknown Author

Because the sinless Savior died my sinful soul is counted free for God the just is satisfied to look on Him and pardon me.

Hebrews 4:15

15 For we have not an high priest which cannot be touched with the feeling of our infirmities; but was in all points tempted like as we are, yet without sin.

Read this passage until you feel you are familiar with it.

Hebrews 4: 15

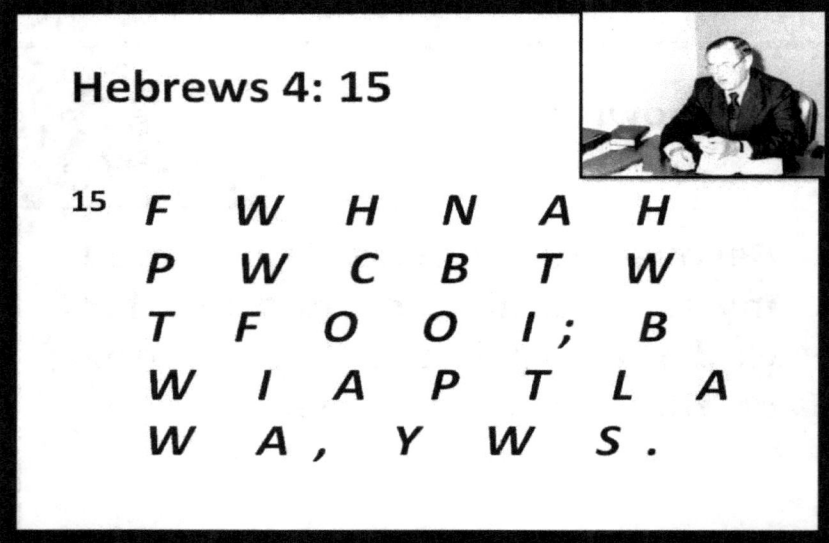

15 *F W H N A H*
P W C B T W
T F O O I; B
W I A P T L A
W A, Y W S.

Say the passage until you can quote it without looking at this aid.

Christ is not a sinner.
I Peter 2:22

I believe that the sinless blood of Jesus Christ is more than adequate to pay the price for my salvation.

Unknown Author

I Peter 2: 22

22 ***Who did no sin, neither was guile found in His mouth:***

Say the passage until you can quote it

from only the address.

I Peter 2: 22

22 ***W D N S, N***
W G F I H M:

Say the passage until you can quote it
from only the address.

Christ is not a sinner.
I John 3:5

Max Lucado

Nails didn't hold God to a cross love did! The Sinless One took on the face of a sinner so we sinners could take on the face of a saint.

I John 3:5

5 ***And ye know that He was manifested to take away our sins; and in Him is no sin.***

Address-verse-address . . .

I John 3:5

5 *A Y K T H W*
M T T A O S;
A I H I N S.

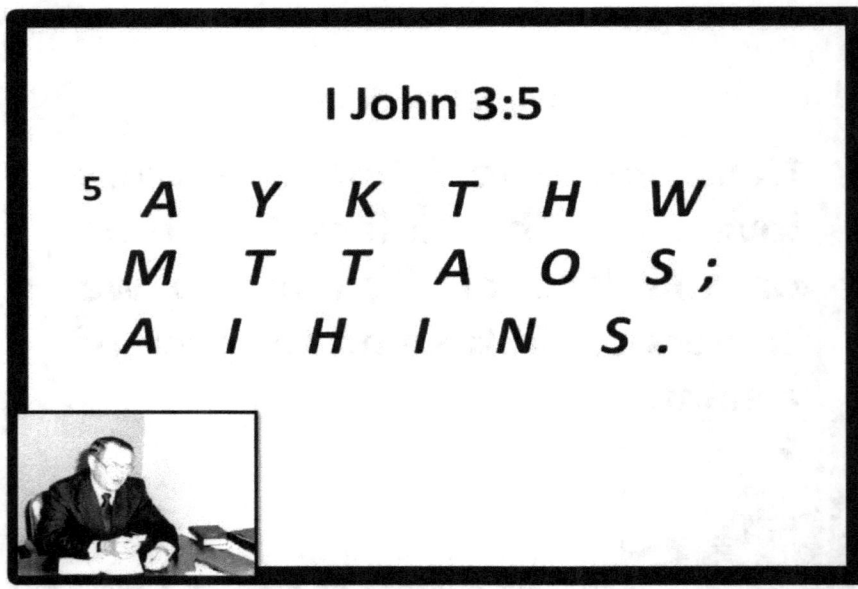

Review . . . Review . . . Review ! ! !

Say the passage until you can quote it
with absolute accuracy.

LESSON 10

Christ died for sinners.
Isaiah 53:6

Billy Sunday

1862 – 1935

Jesus gave His life on the cross for any who will believe. We're not redeemed by silver or gold. Jesus paid for it with His blood.

Isaiah 53:6

6 ***All we like sheep have gone astray; we have turned every one to his own way; and the Lord hath laid on Him the iniquity of us all.***

Preview Isaiah 53:6 here.

Isaiah 53:6

6 *A W L S H G*
A; W H T E O
T H O W; A T
L H L O H T I
O U A.

Download Isaiah 53:6 to your memory here.

Christ died for sinners.
II Corinthians 5:21

Unknown Author

I want to be so full of Jesus that if a mosquito bites me it will fly away singing there is power the blood.

II Corinthians 5:21

21 *For He hath made Him to be sin for us, who knew no sin; that we might be made the righteousness of God in Him.*

II Corinthians 5:21

21 *F H H M H T*
B S F U , W K
N S; T W M B
M T R O G I
H .

. . . a workman that needeth not to be ashamed.

Christ died for sinners.
I Peter 2:24

J. C. Ryle
1816 – 1900

The love of our Lord Jesus Christ towards sinners is strikingly shown in His steady purpose of heart to die for them.

I Peter 2:24

24 *Who His own self bare our sins in His own body on the tree, that we, being dead to sins, should live unto righteousness: by whose stripes ye were healed.*

Read it, read it, read it and read it again.

I Peter 2:24

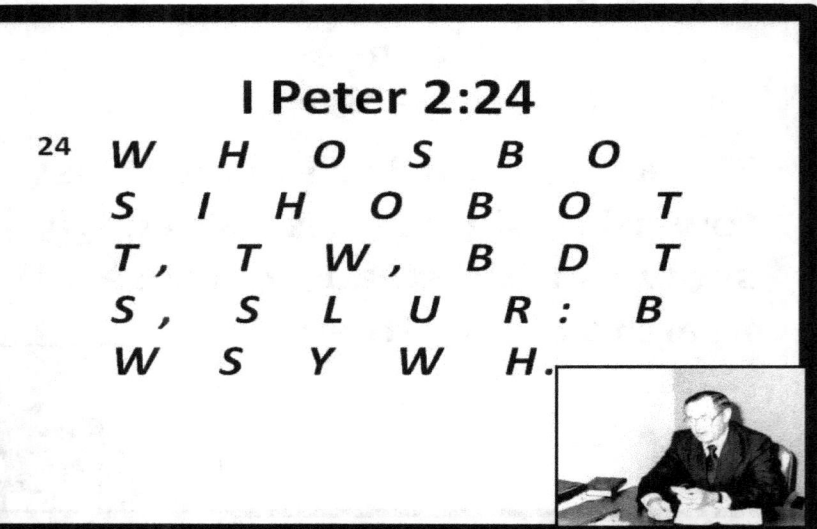

24 *W H O S B O*
S I H O B O T
T, T W, B D T
S, S L U R: B
W S Y W H.

Say it, say it, say it again and quote it.

Christ died for sinners.
I Peter 3:18

D. L. Moody
1837 – 1899

Look at Him at Gethsemane, sweating as it were great drops of blood; look at Him on the cross, crucified between two thieves; hear that piercing cry, "Father, Father, forgive them, they know not what they do." And as you look into that face, as you look into those wounds on His feet or His hands, will you say He has not the power to save you? Will you say He has not the power to redeem you?

I Peter 3:18

18 ***For Christ also hath once suffered for sins, the just for the unjust, that He might bring us to God, being put to death in the flesh, but quickened by the Spirit:***

There is no better use of time than reading God's word.

I Peter 3:18

18 *F C A H O S F*
S, T J F T U,
T H M B U T
G, B P T D I T
F, B Q B T S:

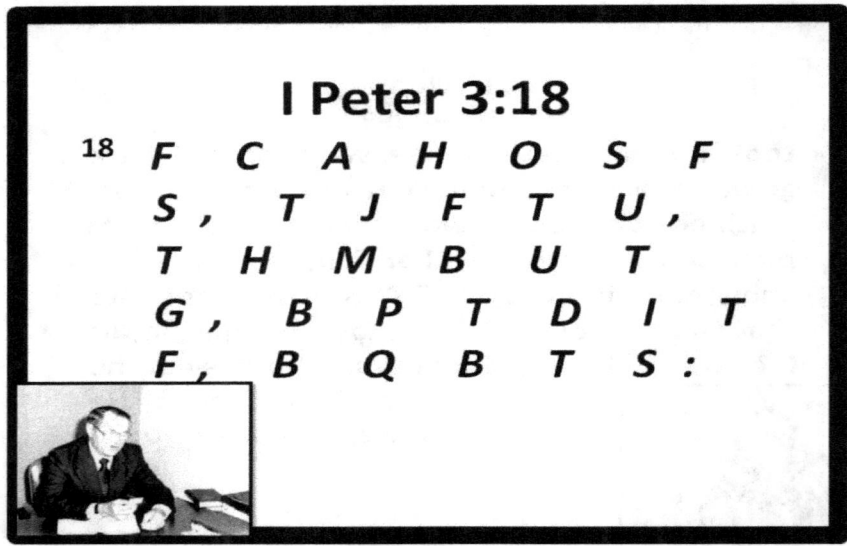

Review . . . Review . . . Review ! ! !

LESSON 11

God is a God of justice and mercy.

Psalm 89:14

Henry Allen Ironside

1876 – 1951

Grace is the very opposite of merit... Grace is not only undeserved favor, but it is favor, shown to the one who has deserved the very opposite.

Psalm 89:14

14 ***Justice and judgment are the habitation of Thy throne: mercy and truth shall go before Thy face.***

God created you with intellect so you can read His word.

Psalm 89:14

14 *J A J A T H*
O T T: M A T
S G B T F.

God created you with a mind to remember His word.

God is a God of justice and mercy.
Psalm 86:15

Charles Haddon Spurgeon
1834 - 1892

God's mercy is so great that you may sooner drain the sea of its water, or deprive the sun of its light, or make space too narrow, than diminish the great mercy of God.

Psalm 86:15

15 But Thou, O Lord, art a God full of compassion, and gracious, longsuffering, and plenteous in mercy and truth.

If you can read and don't what advantage have you on the unlearned?

Psalm 86:15

15 *B T, O L, A A*
G F O C, A
G, L, A P I M
A T.

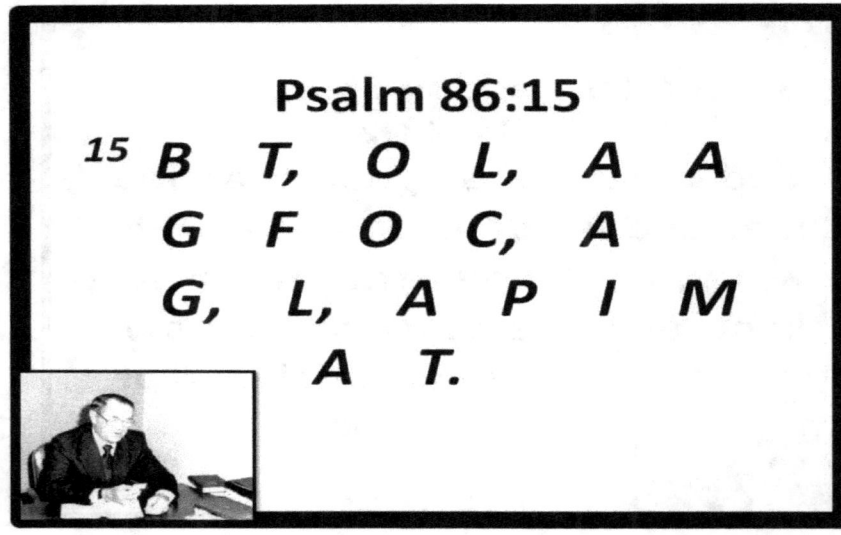

There is nothing better to fill your mind with than God's word.

God is a God of justice and mercy.
Isaiah 53:11

Charles H. Spurgeon
1834 - 1892
In God's case, if He had said in the infinite sovereignty of His absolute will, "I will have no substitute, but each man shall suffer for himself, he who sinneth shall die," none could have murmured. It was grace, and only grace which led the divine mind to say, "I will accept of a substitute. There shall be a vicarious suffering; and My vengeance shall be content, and My mercy shall be gratified."

Isaiah 53:11

11 ***He shall see of the travail of His soul, and shall be satisfied: by His knowledge shall My righteous Servant justify many; for He shall bear their iniquities.***

If Satan can't make bad he'll make you busy.
Make time to read God's word.

Isaiah 53:11

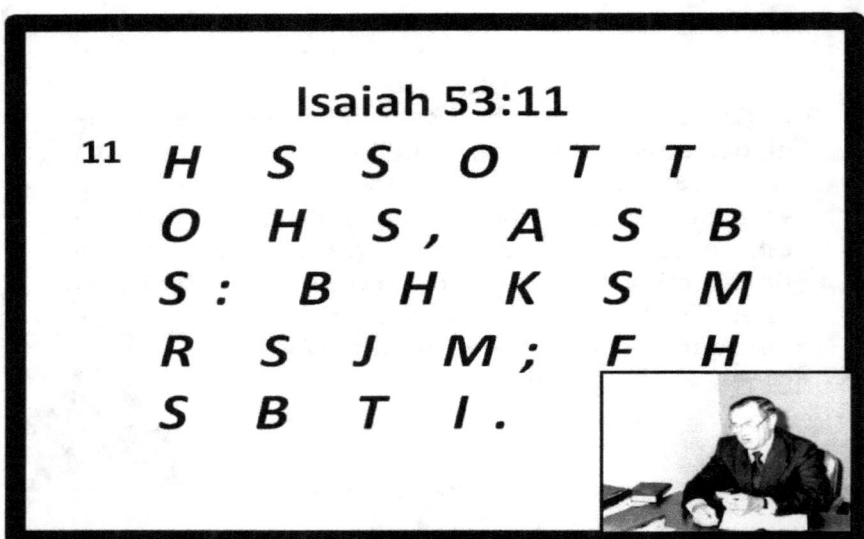

11 ***H S S O T T***
O H S, A S B
S: B H K S M
R S J M; F H
S B T I.

Fill your mind with the "mind of Christ."

God is a God of justice and mercy.
Romans 3:26

Billy Graham

God proved His love on the Cross. When Christ hung, and bled, and died, it was God saying to the world, "I love you."

Romans 3:26

26 ***To declare, I say, at this time His righteousness: that He might be just, and the justifier of him which believeth in Jesus.***

Read . . . Read . . . Read

Romans 3:26

26 *T D, I S, A*
T T H R: T H
M B J, A T J
O H W B I J.

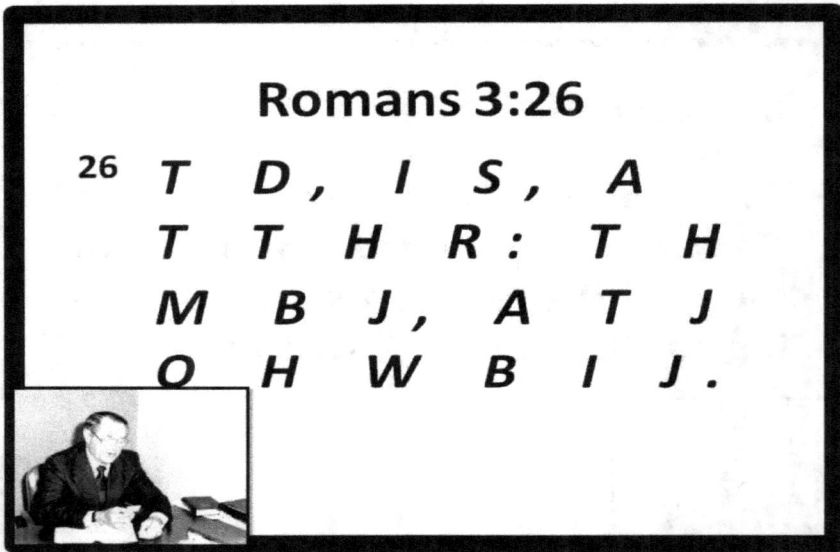

Review . . . Review . . . Review ! ! !

LESSON 12

Repentance and faith are requisites to salvation. (A)

Luke 13:3

Adrian Rogers
1931 - 2005

I believe that a great number of people are going to die and go to hell because they're counting on their religiosity in the church instead of their relationship with Jesus to get them to heaven. They give lip service to repentance and faith, but they've never been born again.

Luke 13:3

3 *I tell you, Nay: but, except ye repent, ye shall all likewise perish.*

Repentance and faith are requisites to salvation.

Luke 13:3

3 *I T Y, N:*
B, E Y R,
Y S A L P.

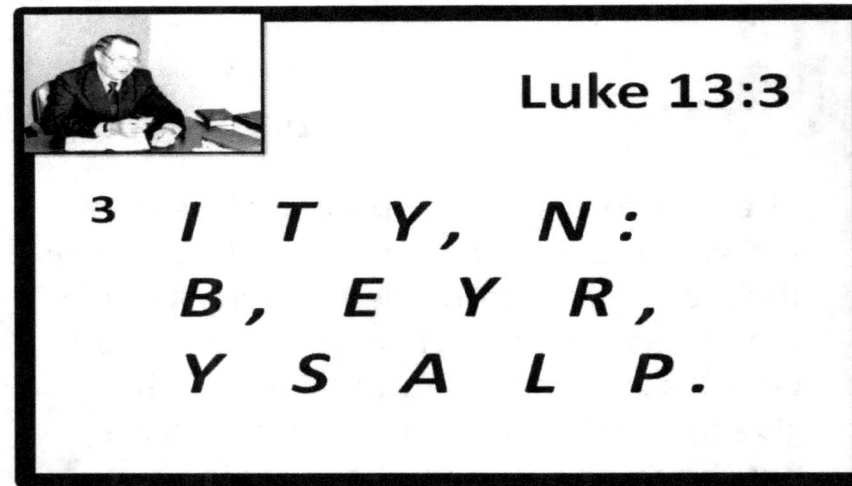

And these words, which I command thee this day, shall be in thine heart:
Deuteronomy 6:6

Repentance and faith are requisites to salvation.
Acts 20:20, 21

Charles H. Spurgeon
1834 - 1892

Another proof of the conquest of a soul for Christ will be found in a real change of life. If the man does not live differently from what he did before, both at home and abroad, his repentance needs to be repented of and his conversion is a fiction.

. . . and shalt talk of them when thou sittest in thine house,
Deuteronomy 6:7b

Acts 20:20, 21

20 ***And how I kept back nothing that was profitable unto you, but have shewed you, and have taught you publickly, and from house to house,***
21 ***Testifying both to the Jews, and also to the Greeks, repentance toward God, and faith toward our Lord Jesus Christ.***

Acts 20:20, 21

20 *A H I K B N T*
W P U Y, B H S
Y, A H T Y P,
A F H T H,
21 *T B T T J, A A*
T T G, R T G,
A F T O L J C.

Repentance and faith are requisites to salvation.
Isaiah 55:7

Charles H. Spurgeon

1834 - 1892

I learn from the Scriptures that repentance is just as necessary to salvation as faith is, and the faith that has not repentance going with it will have to be repented of.

Isaiah 55:7

7 *Let the wicked forsake his way, and the unrighteous man his thoughts: and let him return unto the Lord, and He will have mercy upon him; and to our God, for He will abundantly pardon.*

Review . . . Review . . . Review ! ! !

Isaiah 55:7

7 *L T W F H W,*
A T U M H T:
A L H R U T
L, A H W H M
U H; A T O
G, F H W A
P.

. . . and shalt talk of them when thou sittest in thine house,
Deuteronomy 6:7b

LESSON 13

Repentance and faith are requisites to salvation. (B)

John 3:36

J. C. Ryle

1816 - 1900

True repentance is no light matter. It is a thorough change of heart about sin, a change showing itself in godly sorrow and humiliation - in heartfelt confession before the throne of grace - in a complete breaking off from sinful habits, and an abiding hatred of all sin. Such repentance is the inseparable companion of saving faith in Christ.

John 3:36

36 ***He that believeth on the Son hath everlasting life: and he that believeth not the Son shall not see life; but the wrath of God abideth on him.***

. . . and when thou walkest by the way, and when thou liest down, and when thou risest up. Deuteronomy 6:7c

John 3:36

36 ***H T B O T S***
H E L: A H T
B N T S S N
S L; B T W O

G A O H.

Repentance and faith are requisites to salvation.
Acts 16:30, 31

John Wesley
1703 – 1791

You have nothing to do but to save souls. Therefore spend and be spent in this work. And go not only to those that need you, but to those that need you most. It is not your business to preach so many times, and to take care of this or that society; but to save as many souls as you can; to bring as many sinners as you possibly can to repentance.

Acts 16:30, 31

30 ***And brought them out, and said. Sirs, what must I do to be saved?***
31 ***And they said. Believe on the Lord Jesus Christ, and thou shalt be saved, and thy house.***

Review . . . Review . . . Review ! ! !

Acts 16:30, 31

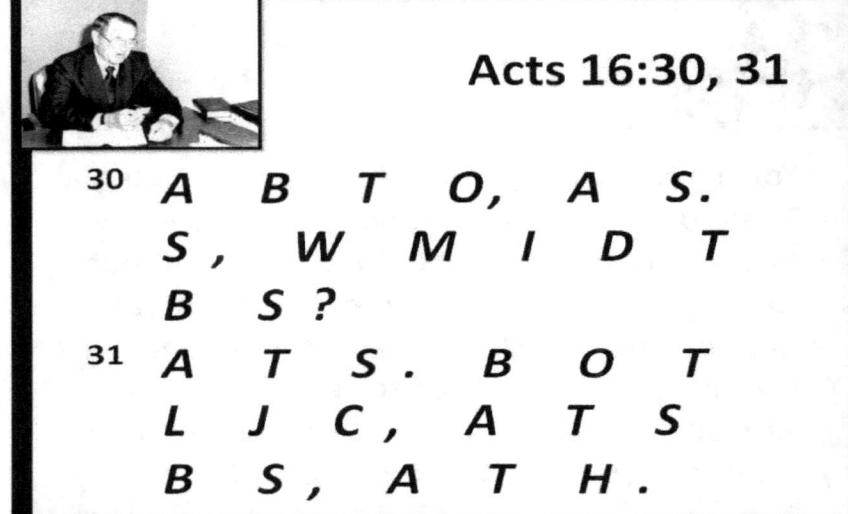

30 ***A B T O, A S.***
S, W M I D T
B S?
31 ***A T S. B O T***
L J C, A T S
B S, A T H.

. . . and they shall be as frontlets between thine eyes.
Deuteronomy 6:8b

Repentance and faith are requisites to salvation.
Galatians 3:26

John Wesley
1703 – 1791

Faith is the divine evidence whereby the spiritual man discerneth God, and the things of God.

Galatians 3:26

26 ***For ye are all the children of God by faith in Christ Jesus.***

Review . . . Review . . . Review

Galatians 3:26

26 *F Y A A T*
C O G B F
I C J.

. . . and they shall be as frontlets between thine eyes.

Deuteronomy 6:8b

LESSON 14

Repentance and faith are requisites to salvation. (C)

John 3:18

J. Vernon McGee

1904 – 1988

You can believe a whole lot of foolish things, but God doesn't want you to do that. He wants your faith to rest upon the Word of God.

John 3:18

18 ***He that believeth on Him is not condemned: but he that believeth not is condemned already, because he hath not believed In the name of the only begotten Son of God.***

Review . . . Review . . . Review

John 3:18

18 *H T B O H I*
N C : B H T B
N I C A , B H
H N B I T N
O T O B S
O G .

9 And thou shalt write them upon the posts of thy house, and on thy gates.
Deuteronomy 6:9

Repentance and faith are requisites to salvation.
John 5:24

R. C. Sproul

The issue of faith is not so much whether we believe in God, but whether we believe the God we believe in.

John 5:24

24 ***Verily, verily, I say unto you, He that heareth My word, and believeth on Him that sent Me, hath everlasting life, and shall not come into condemnation; but is passed from death unto life.***

John 5:24

24 *V, V, I S U Y,*
H T H M W, A
B O H T S M,
H E L, A S N
C I C; B I P F
D U L.

Repentance and faith are requisites to salvation.
Acts 10:43

Andrew Murray
1828 – 1917

Christ will always accept the faith that puts its trust in Him.

Acts 10:43

43 ***To Him give all the prophets witness, that through His name whosoever believeth in Him shall receive remission of sins.***

Review . . . Review . . . Review ! ! !

Acts 10:43

43 ***T H G A T P W, T T H N W B I H S R R O S.***

Repentance and faith are requisites to salvation.
Romans 10:10

J. I. Packer

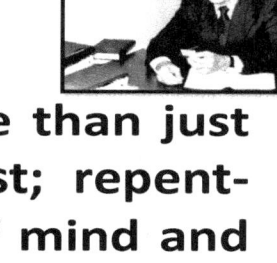

Repentance is more than just sorrow for the past; repentance is a change of mind and heart, a new life of denying self and serving the Savior as king in self's place.

Romans 10:10

10 For with the heart man believeth unto righteousness; and with the mouth confession is made unto salvation.

Review . . . Review . . . Review ! ! !

Romans 10:10

10 ***F W T H M B U R; A W T M C I M U S.***

Review . . . Review . . . Review ! ! !

LESSON 15

The New Birth The necessity of it:

John 3:3, 7

Charles H. Spurgeon

1834 - 1892

No man hath a right to claim God as his Father, unless he feeleth in his soul, and believeth, solemnly, through the faith of God's election, that he has been adopted into the one family of which is in heaven and earth, and that he has been regenerated or born again.

John 3:3, 7

3 ***Jesus answered and said unto him, Verily, verily, I say unto thee. Except a man be born again, he cannot see the kingdom of God...***

7 ***Marvel not that I said unto thee, Ye must be born again.***

{The mystery of it}

The New Birth The necessity of it:

John 3:8

John 3:3,7

3 *J A A S U H, V,*
V, I S U T. E A
M B B A, H C S
T K O G...
7 *M N T I S U T,*
Y M B B A.

The New Birth The necessity of it:
John 3:8

Henry Drummond

1851 - 1897

Even to earnest minds the difficulty of grasping the truth at all has always proved extreme. Philosophically, one scarcely sees either the necessity or the possibility of being born again. Why a virtuous man should not simply grow better and better until in his own right he enter the Kingdom of God is what thousands honestly and seriously fail to understand.

John 3:8

8 ***The wind bloweth where it listeth, and thou hearest the sound thereof, but canst not tell whence it cometh, and whither it goeth: so is every one that is born of the Spirit.***

{The how of it}

Review . . . Review . . . Review ! ! !

John 3:8

8 *T W B W I L , A*
T H T S T, B C
N T W I C, A W
I G : S I E O T
I B O T S.

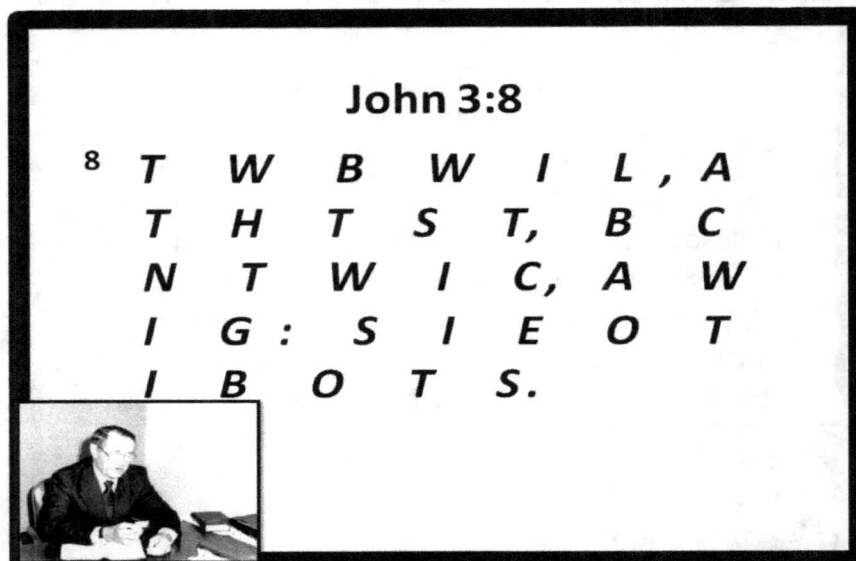

The New Birth The necessity of it:
John 3:14, 15

Watchman Nee
1903 - 1972

Though he may not yet fully experience the meaning of the death of the Lord Jesus, God nevertheless has made him alive together with Christ and he has obtained a new life in the resurrection power of the Lord Jesus. This is new birth.

John 3:14, 15

14 ***And as Moses lifted up the***
serpent in the wilderness, even so
must the Son of Man be lifted up:
15 ***That whosoever believeth in***
Him should not perish, but have
eternal life.

John 3:14, 15

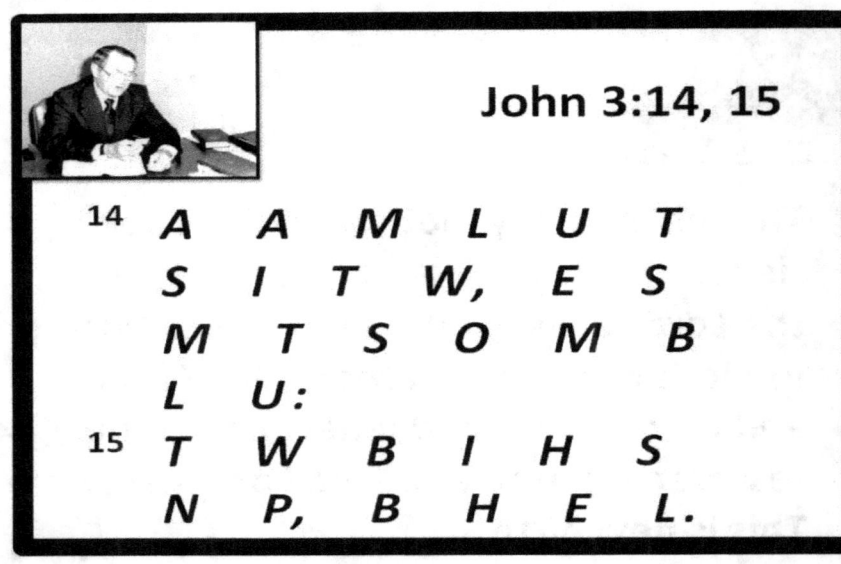

14 ***A A M L U T***
S I T W, E S
M T S O M B
L U:
15 ***T W B I H S***
N P, B H E L.

Review . . . Review . . . Review ! ! !

LESSON 16

Salvation is by grace–a gift of God.

Ephesians 2:8-10

John Stott

1921 - 2011

We must never think of salvation as a kind of transaction between God and us in which He contributes grace and we contribute faith. For we were dead and had to be quickened before we could believe. No, Christ's apostles clearly teach elsewhere that saving faith too is God's gracious gift.

Ephesians 2:8-10

8 For by grace are ye saved through faith; and that not of yourselves: it is the gift of God: 9 Not of works, lest any man should boast. 10 For we are His workmanship, created in Christ Jesus unto good works, which God hath before ordained that we should walk in them.

Review . . . Review . . . Review ! ! !

Ephesians 2:8-10

8 *F B G A Y S*
T F; A T N O Y:
I I T G O G:
9 *N O W, L A M S B.*
10 *F W A H W, C I*
C J U G W, W G
H B O T W S W
I T.

Salvation is by grace–a gift of God.
Titus 3:5

John Newton

1725 - 1807

Amazing grace! How sweet the sound, That saved a wretch like me! I once was lost but now am found, Was blind but now I see.

Titus 3:5

5 ***Not by works of righteousness which we have done, but according to His mercy He saved us, by the washing of regeneration, and renewing of the Holy Ghost:***

Review . . . Review . . . Review ! ! !

Titus 3:5

5 *N B W O R W*
W H D, B A T
H M H S U, B
T W O R, A R
O T H G:

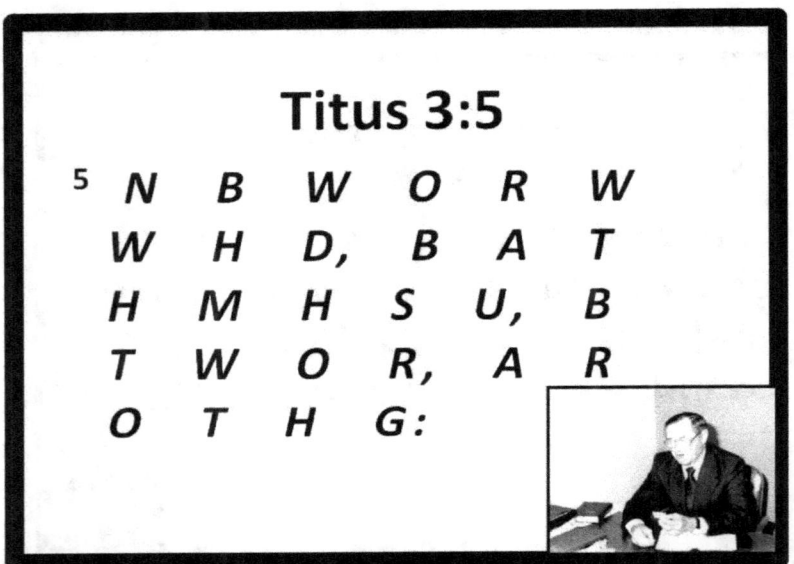

Review . . . Review . . . Review ! ! !

Salvation is by grace–a gift of God.
Ephesians 1:7

John Newton

1725 - 1807

You are coming to a King, Large petitions with you bring, For His grace and power are such, None can ever ask too much.

Ephesians 1:7

7 In whom we have redemption through His blood, the forgiveness of sins, according to the riches of His grace;

Review . . . Review . . . Review ! ! !

Ephesians 1:7

7 *I W W H R T*
H B, T F O S,
A T T R O H G;

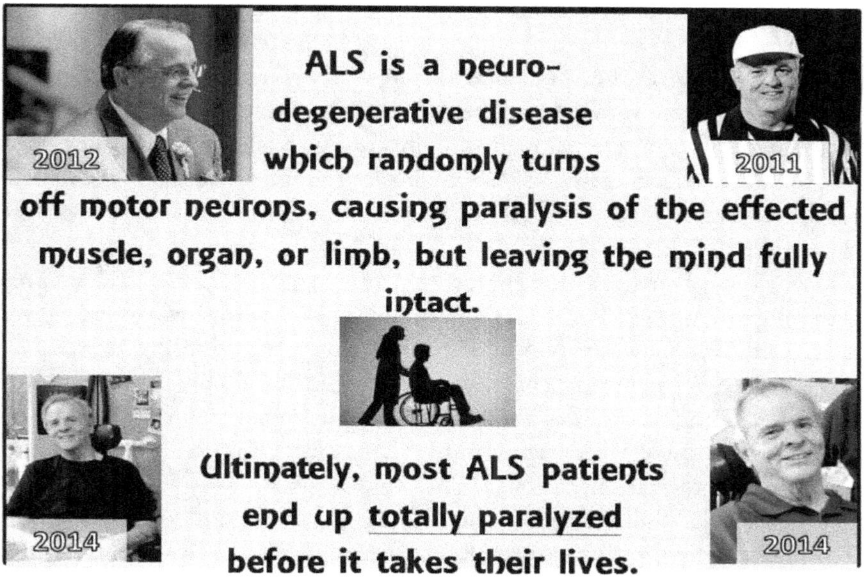
ALS is a neuro-degenerative disease which randomly turns off motor neurons, causing paralysis of the effected muscle, organ, or limb, but leaving the mind fully intact.
2012
2011
2014
2014
Ultimately, most ALS patients end up totally paralyzed before it takes their lives.

ALS AND ME

What do you know about this disease? amyotrophic lateral sclerosis (ALS, or Lou Gehrig's disease).

Four years ago I had only heard of it and really knew nothing about it. Millions of dollars have been raised for research and to assist those living with it and I want to say thank you to all those that have given. Since Lou Gehrig was diagnosed (over 75 years ago) very little has been learned about the cause and there is still no cure.

I would like to share my experience with you. In the summer of 2011 my crew of football officials and I were getting ready for another football season. Studying the rules and running to get in shape. We had a full schedule of regular season games along with several pre-season scrimmages and playoff games ahead of us. But, from the start, I was having trouble breathing and great difficulty running. I finished the most difficult football season of my career. On Sundays I was also having trouble with my voice. No more singing specials and even had to stop singing with the congregation to save my air to preach. It became very hard for me to get up the steps to the pulpit. I was soon using a cane to walk and falls were becoming more frequent. I had always had good health and in my mind I still did. I just did not believe this could be anything serious.

My doctor urged me to have a sleep study. After two sleep studies I was diagnosed with severe sleep apnea. The treatment was to sleep with a Bi-PAP machine. I felt much better and thought I was on my way back. In a few weeks that proved not to be the case. My wife and I were convinced then that the problem had to be my heart but after visiting with my cardiologist and a barrage of test my heart was shown to be fine. A healthy heart is good news but walking with the aid of a cane and struggling to breath showed that I had a problem.

After checking myself into the hospital and two weeks of testing and rehab we were told that I had ALS, a disease for which there is no known cure or treatment. That was March 2013.

Today I am in a wheel chair with no use of my legs at all. I still wear my breathing machine (Bi-PAP) twenty-four hours a day seven days a week. Now I am quickly losing the use of my hands. And I am typing this using my eyes.

ALS is a neuro-degenerative disease which randomly turns off motor neurons, causing paralysis of the effected muscle, organ, or limb, but leaving the mind fully intact. Ultimately, most ALS patients end up totally paralyzed before it takes their lives.

Thanks to all that give to the ALS Association and all who have helped to bring awareness to this disease. And a special thank you to all of those who pray for me. My God is good and all knowing and all powerful and ever present and He loves me and you.

For God so loved the world, that He gave His only begotten Son, that whosoever believeth in Him should not perish, but have everlasting life, John 3:16.

I would also like to encourage everyone to consider giving to these organizations that are committed to meeting the needs of ALS patients in Arkansas. If you're looking to help Arkansans, please give to the Arkansas chapter of the ALS Association or ALS in Wonderland.

Table of Contents

Scripture Index

PUBLISHED by PARABLES
Earthly Stories with a Heavenly Meaning

OUR MISSION

The primary mission of Published By Parables, a Christian publisher, is to publish Contemporary and Classic Christian books from an evangelical perspective that honors Christ and promotes the values and virtues of His Kingdom.

Are You An Aspiring Christian Author?

We fulfill our mission best by providing Christian authors and writers publishing options that are uniquely Christian, quick, affordable and easy to understand -- in an effort to please Christ who has called us to a writing ministry. We know the challenges of getting published, especially if you're a first-time author. God, who called you to write your book, will provide the grace sufficient to the task of getting it published.

We understand the value of a dollar; know the importance of producing a quality product; and publish what we publish for the glory of God.

Surf and Explore our site -- then use our easy-to-use "Tell Us" button
to tell us about yourself and about your book.

We're a one-stop, full-service Christian publisher.
We know our limits. We know our capabilities.
You won't be disappointed.

www.PublishedByParables.com

PUBLISHED *by* PARABLES
Earthly Stories with a Heavenly Meaning

www.ingramcontent.com/pod-product-compliance
Lightning Source LLC
Chambersburg PA
CBHW071736080526
44588CB00013B/2056
* 9 7 8 1 9 4 5 6 9 8 0 0 2 *